SALT & HONEY

AANYA SEN GUPTA

to the days
when the world felt too heavy
and the nights
when the silence was my only friend

to the moments
when my heart ached
and tears were my comfort

to the strength
that grew from my pain
and the light
that emerged from the darkness

this book
is for the parts of me
that broke
and the love
that helped me heal

- Aanya Sen Gupta

Contents

Contents

Contents

Contents

Contents

Foreword

this book

is full of my feelings

written down

    each poem

shows my path

through love and pain

happiness and sadness

    i wrote these words

to heal

to understand

to find peace

    you will see

parts of my heart

in every line

    this is a collection

of emotions

made from my experiences

    i hope

these poems

bring you comfort

and remind you

that you are not alone

Preface

Welcome to this collection of my thoughts and feelings. These poems are like windows into my heart, showing you what I've felt and experienced. I've written them to share a part of myself with you, to let you know that the emotions we go through are things we all understand in our own ways.

In these pages, you'll find love and all its beauty, as well as the pain that sometimes comes with it. You'll read about moments of happiness that fill us up and moments of sadness that make us feel empty. These poems are about life—its ups and downs, its twists and turns.

I've chosen simple words because I want everyone to connect with what I'm saying. Emotions can be complicated, but they're also something we all have in common. So, whether you've experienced similar feelings or you're just starting to explore them, I hope these poems speak to you in a way that makes you feel understood and not alone.

Thank you for joining me on this journey of emotions. May these words bring you comfort, understanding, and a sense of connection.

Acknowledgements

I want to take a moment to reflect on the challenges that have shaped my journey. The days when I faced relentless bullying for aspects of myself I couldn't change, like my skin and acne, were some of the hardest. It felt like everything about me was scrutinized, and it took a toll on my self-esteem. In those moments, my parents and sister stood by me unwaveringly, becoming not just my support system but my pillars of strength. Their love and unwavering belief in me became my guiding light through the darkest times.

When I thought I had experienced heartbreak, I realized it was only heartache until I met him. The pain of feeling shattered and broken to the core was overwhelming. It was during this time that someone unexpected walked into my life and changed everything — Ashley. She's not just a friend; she's a soul sister who has weathered similar storms and emerged stronger. Through her own experiences, she taught me invaluable lessons: how to ignore the noise of negativity, how to make peace with my insecurities, and most importantly, how to cut ties with toxic influences.

Ashley, if you ever come across these words, know that they are filled with immense gratitude. Thank you for being the rock I leaned on, for helping me piece myself back together, and for showing me the power of resilience and friendship. Your presence in my life has been a blessing beyond words, and I cherish every moment of our journey together. I love you bestie.

Prologue

In the quiet moments before the story begins, I want to share a glimpse into what lies ahead. This is a tale of resilience, of navigating the highs and lows of life's rollercoaster. It's about finding strength in vulnerability and discovering that healing often comes from unexpected places.

Through these pages, you'll meet characters shaped by their experiences, just like you and me. They'll laugh, cry, love, and learn, mirroring the complexities of our own journeys. This story is not just theirs; it's a reflection of the human experience — filled with joy, pain, hope, and redemption.

As we embark on this journey together, may you find echoes of your own story intertwined with theirs. For in sharing our narratives, we discover the beauty of our shared humanity and the resilience that resides within us all.

It's all in poetry <3

Welcome to the beginning.

1. Untitled

sting & sweet,
a teardrop on the tongue,
a golden sunrise kiss.
life, a dance
on this tightrope,
salty wounds,
honeyed bliss.

----

cracked skin,
a memory etched in salt,
a single drop,
honey on the fault.

----

bare feet on sand,
ocean whispers a salty song,
a bee's gentle hum,
sweetness lingers all night long.

2. The Unraveling

scars whisper stories,
etched in silver threads,
a tapestry of battles won and lost,
a map of where I've bled.
once, i feared these lines,
proof of vulnerability's sting,
but now, they are constellations,
guiding me where to sing.
for in the unraveling,
i found the strength to mend,
a mosaic of resilience,
a beauty that will never end.

3. The Moon Cycle

she waxes,
a fullness blooming bright,
a beacon for the lost in night.
she wanes,
a sliver thin and frail,
a whisper on the autumn gale.
just like the moon,
my emotions ebb and flow,
a dance of darkness, then aglow.
but even in the deepest dark,
a tiny ember always burns,
a promise that the sun will rise,
and hope in my weary heart returns.

4. The Language of Rain

raindrops tap a rhythm,
on the windowpane so clear,
a symphony for the lonely heart,
washing away all doubt and fear.
each drop, a whispered secret,
from the clouds, a cleansing sigh,
the earth drinks deep, renewed and strong,
mirroring the tears I cry.
for rain is not a sign of sorrow,
but a language of release,
a cleansing fire, a promise made,
that growth will follow after peace.

5. Salt on Skin

tears taste of the ocean,
a constant reminder
of the depths of sorrow
the heart can hold.

6. Unspoken Storms

Eyes, a gray ocean,
reflecting the storm within.
A tightness in my throat,
where words should be, only silence swims.
The sting of salt on my lashes,
a story the wind cannot tell.

7. Broken Compass

North used to be your smile,
east, the warmth of your hand in mine.
Now, I wander lost,
a ship adrift in a sea of brine.
My heart, a compass gone haywire,
spinning with the ache of your absence.

8. Stolen Bloom

a single white rose,
plucked before sunrise,
petals stained,
not with morning dew,
but with a touch unwanted,
a power misused,
innocence ripped,
like the fragile edge of a dream,
thorns now prick my skin,
a constant reminder,
of the garden I can't return to,
where blooms unfurl,
without a price,
where trust isn't a battlefield,
but a haven bathed in honey.

9. Hopeful

though the halls are haunted,
with echoes of your touch,
i open a window,
let the sunlight stream in.
maybe this house can heal,
become a home again,
filled with the ghosts of love,
not just the echoes of pain.

10. We ran

we ran, hearts wild, chasing dreams in flight,
didn't stop to breathe, just you and I, bathed in light.
your hands, a familiar comfort, a place to belong,
but my spirit aches with a silent, unheard song.
beside you, nights whisper stories untold,
a love once vibrant, now turning cold.
we were whirlwinds, chasing futures unseen,
but somewhere along the way, the path grew mean.
your gaze, a mirror reflecting my own pain,
a love lost in the rain.
'cause love is harder, a heavier weight to hold,
life's a different story, not the one we were sold.
who are we to blame for this yearning to roam?
for searching for ourselves, a place to call home?

11. Me

I keep bending barrels
You take aim and shoot
I'm on pins and needles
Your skin's bulletproof.

12. Fragments of Us

we were once whole
pieces of a puzzle
perfectly aligned
but life has a way
of breaking things
scattering fragments
of us
in every direction
each piece a memory
each shard a scar
we carried them
like burdens
like lessons
etched deep into our skin
we've been through storms
that tore us apart
through nights
drenched in tears
through moments
of unbearable silence
where all we could hear
was the sound of our own
breaking hearts

but here we are
standing tall
amidst the ruins
of what once was
we picked up the pieces
one by one
stitched them together
with threads of resilience
with hands that shook
but never gave up
we are the sum
of our fragments
the beauty in the broken
the strength in the scars
we have healed
through the pain
transformed by it
we stand tall
not in spite of it
but because of it.

13. The Silent Sacrifice

they say superheroes
wear capes
but mine
wore tired eyes
and calloused hands
my mother
held our world together
with whispers
of strength
and quiet sacrifice
she never asked
for anything in return
just the smile
on our faces
was enough.

14. The Unseen Hero

my father
worked late nights
and early mornings
his dreams
were wrapped in our futures
he carried the weight
of our world
on his shoulders
never once
letting it show
i saw him
leave everything
just to be there
in moments
when i needed him most
he is my hero
not for the battles
he fought
but for the love
he gave.

15. The Gentle Strength

my mother's hands
have known hard work
and gentle touch
in every meal she cooked
in every wound she healed
she held us
through our darkest nights
her strength
a quiet river
flowing beneath
our feet.

16. Lessons in Silence

my father taught me
lessons in silence
in the way he stood tall
against the storms
in the way he faced
life's trials
with a steady heart
he never spoke
of the burdens he bore
but his actions
whispered
of courage and love
stronger than words.

17. The Warm Embrace

there was a time
when my world
fell apart
and it was my mother's arms
that pulled me back together
her embrace
was a shield
against the coldness
of the world
a place
where i could find
warmth and safety.

18. A Father's Love

my father's love
was never loud
it was the quiet assurance
of his presence
the silent support
in times of need
he was the anchor
in the storm
the unwavering hand
that guided me
through the roughest seas.

19. The Weight of Their Love

they carried
the weight of the world
on their shoulders
so we could stand tall
with every wrinkle
etched into their skin
they wore their sacrifices
like badges of honor
silent struggles
hidden behind
tired eyes and warm smiles
they gave us everything
even when they had nothing
we never saw
the nights they stayed up
worrying, planning, praying
we only saw the morning sun
and their unwavering strength
we may never
fully understand
the depths of their love
but in every action

we find their devotion

they are the roots

that ground us

the arms that lift us

the hearts that keep us beating.

20. Invisible Heroes

in the quiet
before dawn breaks
they rise with the sun
unseen, unnoticed
every meal cooked
every lesson taught
every wound kissed
they are the silent
heroes of our lives
their dreams put on hold
to build ours
their tears hidden
so we could smile
they taught us
kindness, strength, love
through gentle words
and selfless acts
their love is a quiet force
steady and enduring
a lighthouse guiding us
through life's storms
we are who we are
because of them

and yet, their sacrifices

often go unsung

let us cherish

these invisible heroes

for in their quiet love

we find our greatest strength.

21. Love

"What does love mean to you?" my mum asks eight year old me with a gentle smile.

I pause, thinking for a moment, then brighten up as I respond, "Love is like the bond you and dad have. It's like the way you hold hands when you walk together, always supporting each other. Love is when you laugh together, even at silly jokes. It's the hugs that make everything better, and the way you look at each other with so much kindness. Love is knowing that no matter what, you'll always be there for each other, just like you are for me."

Love, after facing many heartbreaks, takes on a deeper meaning. It's a journey of growth and self-discovery, where pain becomes a teacher and scars turn into stories of resilience. Love is not just about the highs of happiness and butterflies; it's also about the lows of disappointment and tears. It's understanding that love can be messy, imperfect, and sometimes heartbreaking, but it's still worth experiencing.

Through heartbreaks, I've learned that love is about acceptance and forgiveness, both for others and myself. It's about letting go of expectations and embracing the reality of each moment. Love is finding beauty in vulnerability and strength in letting wounds heal. It's about finding balance between passion and reason, between holding on and letting someone go.

Despite the pain, love remains a source of hope and joy. It's the laughter shared with friends, the warmth of family bonds, and the moments of connection that remind us of our humanity. Love is a tapestry woven from experiences, each thread contributing to the intricate pattern of our lives. And even in the darkest moments, love shines as a beacon of light, guiding us forward with courage and resilience.

So, when my mom asks what love means to me now, I'd say it's a journey of self-discovery, of learning to love and forgive myself as much as I love others. It's finding strength in vulnerability and courage in letting go when needed. Love is not just about romantic relationships; it's about the love I have for my family, friends, and most importantly, for myself.

22. Because of love

i used to think love was enough
to fix everything
to heal all wounds
to make the world right again
but i was wrong
love is not a bandaid
it is not a cure-all
it is not the answer to every question
love can be selfish
it can be blinding
it can make you forget
everything and everyone else
i lost friends
because i was too consumed
by my own love story
to see theirs
i was so busy chasing my own happy ending
that i forgot to be there for them
when they needed me most
and now those friendships
are broken, maybe beyond repair
a cautionary tale
of what happens when you let love

cloud your judgement
and your loyalty

23. Love is...

love is not a fairytale
it's not roses and chocolates
and happily ever after
love is messy
it's fighting and making up
it's compromise and sacrifice
love is seeing someone at their worst
and still thinking they're beautiful
it's holding their hand through the darkness
and being their light when they can't see
love is not perfect
it's not always easy
but it's worth it
because when you find that person
who makes your heart skip a beat
who makes you feel alive
who loves you for exactly who you are
there's nothing else like it in the world

24. Unconditional Love

Love knows no bounds, it's always there,
A constant presence, beyond compare.
It's in the laughter of a child's play,
And in the stars that light our way.
Love forgives, it understands,
It holds us close with gentle hands.
Through every trial, it remains strong,
A melody of hope in life's song.
Love's beauty lies in its simplicity,
A silent force, yet full of empathy.
It speaks in whispers, soft and clear,
Love's essence, forever near.

25. Innocence lost

In the garden of innocence, we played,
Hearts unburdened, laughter unafraid.
But as time weaved its intricate design,
Innocence faded, leaving pain behind.
Love, a fragile flower, bloomed and wilted,
Promises broken, emotions stilted.
Yet in this journey of joy and sorrow,
We found solace in a brighter tomorrow

26. Heartbreak

heartbreak is a special kind of pain
it cuts deeper than any blade
leaves scars that never fully heal
it's like having your heart ripped out
stomped on, and then shoved back in
still beating, still alive
but forever changed
heartbreak is the death of a dream
the shattering of an illusion
the realization that love is not enough
it's the loneliest feeling in the world
being surrounded by people who love you
and still feeling utterly alone
heartbreak is the price we pay
for opening our hearts
for letting someone in
for daring to love
but it's also the price of growth
of learning
of becoming who we're meant to be
so we pick up the pieces
stitch our hearts back together
and keep moving forward

because that's all we can do

27. Echoes

the silence in this room
used to be filled with laughter,
yours and mine, bouncing off the walls.
now it echoes hollow,
a cavern carved by your absence.
i trace the outline of your ghost
on the sheets, a memory imprint,
a map of where you used to be.
the air is thick with the scent
of your cologne, a cruel reminder
that you are everywhere and nowhere.
my heart, a shattered kaleidoscope,
reflects fractured pieces of us,
a million moments spun to dust.
i am a puzzle with missing pieces,
searching for a shape i can no longer hold.

28. Stitching the Sun

tears, salty and endless,

stain my cheeks, a constant thrumming rain.

they fall for the promises whispered,

now broken shards on the floor.

my breath hitches, a sob escapes,

a raw, primal sound of a love lost.

grief claws at my throat, a feral beast,

choking on the ghost of what we were.

but somewhere, beneath the wreckage,

a sliver of light flickers.

a stubborn hope, a fragile bud,

pushing through the cracks of despair.

i gather the broken pieces of myself,

like scattered pearls on the beach.

with trembling hands, i stitch them together,

a tapestry woven with heartache and healing.

the sun, a silent witness, peeks through the clouds,

a reminder that even after the darkest night,

dawn will break.

i may be forever marked by this loss,

but the scars will become a map,

guiding me towards a love that mends,

a future where my shattered heart blooms again.

29. The Space Between Us

we used to fit together,
like puzzle pieces carved for each other.
but something shifted, a fault line grew,
and now we are continents adrift.
conversations turned to empty monologues,
touch turned to a cold, distant space.
love, once a vibrant flame, now flickers,
a dying ember in the wind.
the distance between us, a chasm vast,
unbridgeable by whispered apologies,
or promises etched in fading ink.
letting go feels like a betrayal,
a surrender to the inevitable.
but holding on to a broken dream,
only hurts us both.
i release you with a bittersweet sigh,
a teardrop for what could have been.
may we find healing in the space between us,
and learn to love ourselves whole again.

30. The Moon Weeps

the moon, usually a silent observer,
tonight weeps with me.
her cratered face, a reflection
of the hollow ache in my chest.
i walk the streets, a ghost in the city,
searching for solace in the neon glow.
but every laugh, every embrace,
sharpens the edges of my loneliness.
strangers brush past, oblivious to my storm,
their hurried lives a distant melody.
i yearn for the warmth of your hand in mine,
a comfort now lost in the night.

31. The Book with Torn Pages

i reread our story,
written in ink stained with tears.
each page, a cherished memory,
now a painful reminder of what's gone.
i trace your name with a trembling finger,
the letters blurring through a veil of sorrow.
our journey, a fairytale with a tragic twist,
a love story left unfinished.

32. The Garden After Rain

the storm has passed, leaving behind
a world washed clean, a tender silence.
my heart, a battered garden,
weeps with the rain-soaked rose.
petals lie scattered on the ground,
bruised and broken, their beauty marred.
but beneath the wreckage, life persists,
a small green shoot pushing through the grime.
i tend to the wounded flowers,
with gentle hands and a hopeful heart.
the path to healing will be long,
but with each sunrise, a new bloom will arise.

33. The Ghost in the Coffee Shop

steam curls from my mug,

a wisp of warmth against the chill

of the empty seat across from me.

we used to linger here for hours,

lost in conversations laced with laughter,

sharing dreams over coffee and croissants.

now, the silence screams in my ears,

broken only by the clatter of spoons

and the murmur of strangers.

i reach for your hand, a phantom limb,

grasping at the memory of your touch.

the scent of your cologne lingers faintly,

a cruel trick of the mind.

i close my eyes, and for a moment,

i see your smile, hear your voice.

but the world snaps back into focus,

leaving me with the bitter aftertaste of loss.

34. The Language of Scars

they map my body, these jagged lines,

a silent story etched in crimson ink.

each scar whispers of battles fought,

of love lost and lessons learned.

some are faint, a reminder of fleeting pain,

while others carve deep, a constant ache.

but they are not flaws, these marks of resilience,

a testament to the strength that lies within.

i hope to wear them like badges of honor,

to prove that I have fallen, but risen again.

believe for scars are not the end, but a beginning,

a chapter in the story of my beautiful, broken self.

35. Self hate

i used to look in the mirror
and all i saw was flaws
the acne on my skin
the curves of my body
i hated everything about myself
my nose, my thighs, my smile
i thought if i could just change
everything would be better
but no matter how much weight i lost
or how much makeup i put on
the self-hate never went away
it was a voice in my head
constantly criticizing
constantly putting me down
you're not good enough
you'll never be enough
you're fat, ugly, unlovable
but that voice was wrong
i am enough
i am worthy of love
exactly as i am
my body is not a flaw
it's a work of art

a temple that houses my soul
and i am learning to love it
to appreciate it
to treat it with kindness and respect
because self-hate is a prison
and i refuse to be its prisoner anymore

36. Cracked Mirror

i stare into the glass, a stranger stares back.
eyes hollow, reflecting a soul under attack.
the face i see, a canvas marred with flaws,
a distorted image, trapped in self-made laws.
each blemish, a mountain, every scar, a sin.
my mind a cruel critic, letting nothing in.
the voice inside whispers, "you'll never be enough,"
a relentless echo, steeped in bitter stuff.

37. Cage of Comparison

scrolling through lives, perfect and bright,

a curated world, bathed in filtered light.

their laughter rings hollow, their smiles too wide,

a constant reminder of all that I hide.

i shrink in the shadows, unseen, unheard,

my worth measured in likes, a fleeting, absurd

obsession with validation, a never-ending chase.

their achievements a mirror, reflecting my disgrace.

the cage of comparison, a prison I've built,

bars forged from envy, with self-doubt spilt.

i yearn to break free, to see my own worth,

but the bars hold me captive, a burden of birth.

38. Wilted Flower

i used to bloom, vibrant and bold,
petals unfurled, a story untold.
but the sun grew harsh, the rain turned to sleet,
my spirit withered, beneath a bitter defeat.
now I stand fragile, a wilted display,
colors faded, beauty gone astray.
the life force within me struggles to fight,
choked by the weeds of self-doubt and self-hate's blight.
i yearn for the gardener, a hand reaching out,
to nurture the spark, extinguish the doubt.
but the fear holds me rooted, unable to grow,
a prisoner of darkness, where only shadows flow.

39. Dust

I wake each morning, coated in a film,
not of sleep, but of self-loathing's grime.
A heavy layer, blurring the lines,
between who I am, and what my mind defines.
The mirror reflects a distorted face,
every flaw magnified, a brutal embrace.
I scrub and I cleanse, but the feeling remains,
a constant reminder of the self I disdain.
This internal storm, a dust devil within,
churning doubts and fears, a relentless din.
It chokes out the light, the beauty unseen,
leaving a desolate landscape, barren and mean.

40. The Unworthy Vessel

My body, a temple, they say, a sacred space.
But it feels like a prison, a cage of disgrace.
I carry my burdens, a weight on my frame,
a burden of self-hate, whispered in my name.
Every curve, every line, a source of despair,
a constant reminder of all I can't bear.
Unworthy of love, unworthy of touch,
just a vessel of flaws, loved far too much (a lie, a crutch).
I yearn to shatter this form, to break free,
to shed these constraints and finally be.
But fear holds me captive, a paralyzing chain,
trapped in this vessel, tormented by pain.

41. The Broken Record

The same song plays on repeat, a broken refrain,
a chorus of negativity, driving me insane.
"You're not good enough," it screams in my ear,
a relentless critic, fueling my deepest fear.
I try to mute the volume, turn the dial down low,
but the record keeps spinning, a constant undertow.
It drags me back to the darkness, the pit of despair,
where self-hate festers, a burden I bear.

42. The empty chair

I pull up a chair, worn and familiar,
a place reserved for a guest so unclear.
This chair, a symbol of a love long gone,
a phantom presence, where laughter once shone.
I set the table for two, a silent plea,
hoping the guest will return and sit with me.
But the chair remains empty, the plate a stark white,
a stark reminder of a love lost in the night.
The silence screams questions, unanswered and raw,
"Was I enough?" it echoes, a gnawing claw.
Self-doubt creeps in, a serpent unfurling,
whispering tales of a love undeserving.
I gather the plates, the remnants of a dream,
a single tear falling, a glistening stream.
But as I clear the table, a resolve starts to bloom,
to fill the empty chair, with love for this room.

43. The Moth and the Flame

I am like a moth, drawn to the flame of despair,
circling endlessly, consumed by the air
thick with negativity, a moth to its doom.
The self-destructive fire, lighting the room.
The voices ignite me, whisper sweet lies,
of validation withheld, and a love that denies.
I dance with the flames, a hypnotic embrace,
blinded by darkness, losing my pace.
But a flicker of hope, a distant, faint light,
pulls me away from the fire, a chance to take flight.
The path to healing, a struggle I face,
to break free from the flames, and find a brighter space.

44. Insecurities

we all have them
those little voices in our heads
whispering doubts and fears
you're not smart enough
you're not pretty enough
you're not good enough
insecurities are like weeds
they creep in and take over
choking out our confidence
they make us second-guess ourselves
doubt our abilities
hide our true selves away
but insecurities are also a liar
they tell us we're not worthy
when in reality, we are
we are smart, we are strong
we are beautiful, inside and out
and the more we feed our insecurities
the more power we give them
but we can choose to starve them
to silence those voices
and let our true selves shine

it's not easy, but it's worth it
because when we conquer our insecurities
we unlock our full potential

45. Cracks

these stretch marks,
a map of where I've grown,
a battleground
where my body bloomed.
insecurity whispers,
flaws etched in pale lines,
but resilience tells a story,
of strength that intertwined.
these cracks,
not imperfections,
but battle scars of beauty,
a testament to my functions.

46. The Mirror Lies

the mirror,
a cold, reflective pane,
shows a distorted image,
washed in self-doubt's rain.
it whispers lies,
of flaws that don't exist,
a warped perception,
a cruel, judging twist.

47. "You'll never be complete"

I stare at my reflection
And she stares back -
A distorted fabric
Of flaws and cracks
The doubts creep in
Like spiders weaving webs,
Ensnaring my thoughts
With every thread.
Am I pretty enough?
Smart enough? Worthy?
The questions swarm
Like bees in my belly.
I pinch at the softness,
The dimples, the scars,
Wishing to peel off
My insecure mars.
But the doubts only grow
When I scatter their seeds -
A garden of gremlins
To answer my needs.
I know in my heart
I am precious and deep.

Yet the whispers persist:
"You'll never be complete."

48. Fly high

She irons her hair,
Straights every curl,
Presses the wrinkles
Of who she's been - girl
To woman, emerging
From cocoon of youth.
Yet her wings feel broken,
Unworthy of truth.
The knots in her core
Can't be simply erased.
The mirror reminds her
Of all she's defaced.
She wishes for softness,
A gentler embrace,
Rather than this mask
She must wear on her face.
But the world judges harshly,
By cover not words.
So she straightens her crown
Though inside she's a bird
With feathers in disarray,
Longing to fly
Without all these knots

Telling her, "You'll never fly high."

49. Self-Harm

i used to think hurting myself
was the only way to feel alive
to let the pain out
to punish myself for being broken
i would carve my skin
with razors and knives
watch the blood drip down
like a crimson river
i thought if i hurt myself enough
on the outside
it would numb the ache
on the inside
but all it did was leave scars
reminders of the battles
i fought with my own mind
the war i'm still waging
against my own body
self-harm is not the answer
it's a temporary fix
a bandaid on a bullet wound
it doesn't make the pain go away
it just hides it for a little while

but i'm learning to find other ways
to cope with the darkness
to let it out without hurting myself
because i am worth more than this
i am strong
i am a survivor
and i will not let my trauma
define me.

50. Scars Speak

In the quiet of night,
My scars whisper stories untold,
Of battles fought within,
Of pain, so deep, so cold.
Each mark a silent cry,
A plea for help unseen,
Yet in the darkness, they shine bright,
Testaments to where I've been.

51. Bleeding Heart

My heart bleeds in shades of red,
Invisible wounds that no one sees,
Each drop a tale of inner dread,
A silent plea for some release.
I paint my pain with crimson hues,
On skin that bears the weight of sorrow,
A canvas of broken dreams and bruised,
A story of a soul's tomorrow.

52. Scars Like Constellations

skin a map,
etched with battles fought
in the quiet dark.
each line, a story untold,
a constellation of pain,
guiding lost stars home.

53. Whispers

the blade whispers promises,
a twisted lullaby,
soothing the storm within.
but the scars they leave,
scream a truth
even silence can't deny.

54. Blunt

the urge, a dull ache
not a sharp scream this time.
a yearning for a familiar sting,
a release in the red bloom.
but even the blade feels tired,
worn thin by the battles
it can no longer win.

55. Not This Time

fingertips trace the familiar map,
the raised terrain, a memory sharp.
but tonight, a whisper stronger,
a voice that says, "This time, no."
a tiny spark of defiance,
a fragile hope for a different tomorrow.

56. Counting Scars

each line a number,
a tally of the wars waged.
a twisted math,
where pain becomes currency,
and suffering the only wage.
but tonight, a different count,
the breaths I take,
a promise to find a better way.

57. Mirror, Mirror

eyes that used to sparkle,
now dulled by a storm within.
the reflection, a stranger,
a distorted image of who I've been.
but behind the mask of pain,
a flicker of fight,
a whisper, "You are beautiful,
even in the darkest night."

58. my art

my body is not a prison
it's a temple
a work of art
a miracle
but sometimes it feels like a cage
trapping me inside
a body I don't recognize
body dysmorphia is a beast
that distorts my reflection
makes me see flaws where there are none
it tells me I'm fat, ugly, unworthy
when in reality, I am strong, beautiful, enough
it's a voice in my head
constantly criticizing, never satisfied
but I am learning to silence that voice
to see myself through the eyes of love
to appreciate my body for all that it is
my body is not perfect
it has scars and stretch marks
curves and imperfections
but it is mine
and it is worthy of love and respect

I am learning to treat my body
with kindness and compassion
to nourish it, move it, honor it
because my body is not a flaw
it is a miracle
a testament to my strength and resilience
and I will not let body dysmorphia
take that away from me.

59. Depression

depression is a heavy weight
on my shoulders, in my heart
a darkness that seeps into my bones
and makes it hard to breathe
some days, it's all I can do
to get out of bed, to face the world
the simplest tasks feel like climbing mountains
and the future feels bleak and hopeless
depression is a liar
it tells me I'm worthless, a burden
that no one cares, that I'll never be happy
but depression is also a teacher
it's shown me the depths of my own strength
the resilience of the human spirit
because even on the darkest days
when the weight feels too heavy to bear
I find the courage to keep going
to reach out for help, to lean on loved ones
to remind myself that this too shall pass
depression is not my identity
it's a challenge I face, a battle I fight
but it does not define me

I am more than my mental illness

I am a warrior, a survivor, a work in progress

and I will not let depression win.

60. Broken Pieces

I am a puzzle of shattered dreams,
Broken pieces, silent screams.
Each fragment a story untold,
A journey of pain, a heart cold.
Smiles painted, masks worn,
Inside, a storm fiercely torn.
Tears hidden, fears denied,
A facade of strength, a fragile pride.
Words unspoken, wounds unseen,
A labyrinth of thoughts, a silent scream.
Lost in the maze of my mind,
Seeking solace, but peace hard to find.

61. Allergic- clide

It got old, following you around
Trying to get you to talk to me
And it got old, wanted to let you in
But you didn't want to fix shit

I've been burned before ya
But there's just something about us
That doesn't hurt to give this up

62. Paper cuts

words like paper cuts
invisible
but stinging
doubts whispered
in the dead of night
festering in my mind
a slow bleed
of confidence
i have to breathe
slow
and heal.

63. To-Do Lists

endless scribbles
on crumpled paper
tasks multiplying
like rabbits in the night
a constant pressure
to achieve
to conquer
the blank spaces
a battle won
each one crossed out
but the list
never truly ends
is this enough?

64. Breathe

lungs constricting
air a distant memory
panic a tight fist
around my chest
i count to ten
inhale the quiet
exhale the storm
slowly
i find my rhythm again
a small victory
but a victory nonetheless

65. Social Static

a room full of voices
laughing, buzzing
but my mind
is a radio with bad reception
static drowns them out
afraid to reach out
afraid of the silence
after the words are gone
a smile plastered on
hoping no one sees the fear.

66. Comparison Trap

scrolling, scrolling
perfect lives on display
accomplishments, smiles
a pit forming in my stomach
not good enough
never good enough
i close the app.

67. Body Betrayal

a knot in my stomach
a sudden sweat
my own body a traitor
against my will
fighting a battle
on a battlefield
of my own creation
learning to trust
and find peace
within the chaos.

68. Mirrored Tears

Mirror, mirror, on the wall,
Why these spots that stain me small?
Whispers echo, laughter stings,
"Ugly skin," their playground sings.
Brown eyes welling, salty stream,
Wishing I could be a dream.
Not of beauty, that's not true,
Just unseen, like morning dew.

69. Colours of Me

Skin like sunshine, warm and bright,
But laughter fades in darkened light.
"Too dark," they taunt, a cruel decree,
Wishing I could be like them, you see.
But colors paint a world so grand,
From sunrise hues to ocean sand.
My skin, a canvas, strong and true,
Holds the beauty shining through.

70. Moonlit Mirror

mirror, at night, the only one who sees,
the craters etched, a war my skin can't appease.
their whispers echo, "pizza face," they say,
stealing the shine I try to hold all day.
but the moon understands, its face pocked too,
beauty found in imperfections, shining through.
one day, my confidence will eclipse their taunts,
leaving scars a reminder, not permanent haunts.

71. Tears on Lotion

cotton ball whispers, can't erase the pain,
red blooms erupt, a daily summer rain.
bathroom mirror, a battlefield I see,
tears mix with lotion, a silent plea.
"Ugly," they laugh, a punch to my gut,
hiding my face, wishing I could shut
out the world that sees only the flaw,
not the brave heart fighting this war.

72. Hidden Smile

Lunchbox shut tight, a smile I hide,
Red dots erupt, a source of derision's tide.
Mirrors avoided, a painful sight,
Wishing for smooth skin, bathed in moonlight.
Their laughter cuts, a constant ache,
Longing for silence, a peaceful break.
But a fire burns, fierce and bright,
I won't let them dim my inner light.
One day, I'll bloom, a radiant flower,
Ignoring their whispers, embracing my power.
My skin's a story, a journey I own,
Beautiful, strong, never alone.

73. Always

I always knew our break was my medicine
I couldn't stay away cause I love that feeling
Dream too much, I wanna feel the pain
Too many feelings, don't wanna feel it
Please don't fall for me
Could you stay 'til the morning?

74. I saw london without you

Its been three months since I saw you
Just a few texts here and there
I saw you're on a beach somewhere
I think I forgot to tell you
I found that list on my phone,
Of places in London you wanted to go
Those tourist shops around camden town
take a late night ride on the underground
See the gardens and drink warm beer
I know you would die,if you knew I was here
I feel so helpless and I feel so far away
If you knew where I was I wonder what you'd say
I feel guilty and I don't know how to tell you
I saw London without you
Everything here makes me miss you
I can picture us
Still in love
Holding hands on a rooftop bus
I haven't posted any pictures
Cause there's a part of me
That still believes
Ill bring you back to these

75. I trusted you

i trusted you with my heart
with my secrets and dreams
you held them in your hands
and i thought they were safe
but you shattered them
like glass falling to the ground
you were my everything
my sun, my moon, my stars
but now i see the truth
you were a storm
that destroyed my calm
i believed in your promises
in the sweetness of your words
but they were lies
wrapped in honey
deceit in disguise
how do i pick up the pieces
of a heart that was whole
only to be broken
by the one it loved most?

76. Betrayal

your betrayal cut deep
like a knife through my soul
i never saw it coming
the pain you would bestow
i gave you my trust
my love, my everything
but you threw it all away
for a moment of nothing

77. Slow

Someone left me with a broken heart
That I passed on to someone
And broke a new one apart
Things can be good enough
Still not enough

78. The other women

she was the other woman
the one you chose over me
and now i am left
questioning my worth
i see her in my dreams
her face, her smile
and i wonder
what does she have
that i do not
i compare myself to her
every curve, every flaw
and i feel small
in the shadow of her allure
did she laugh at your jokes
the way i used to
did she make you feel alive
in a way i never could
the insecurity seeps in
like a poison to my soul
and i struggle to remember
the person i once was
i gave you everything
my love, my trust

but you found something in her
that i could not provide
how do i heal
when my self-worth is shattered
by the thought of her
in your arms

79. Love and pain

you asked me
what love feels like
and i told you
it feels like the ocean
crashing against my heart
sometimes gentle
sometimes fierce
always there
you said
it sounds beautiful
but does it hurt
i looked into your eyes
and said
love is the most beautiful pain
i have ever known.

80. Healing

i thought
i would never
be whole again
that the pieces
of my broken heart
would stay scattered
forever
but time
has a gentle way
of mending wounds
and now
i carry my scars
like a map
of where i have been
and who i have become

81. Heart "ache"

they say
time heals all wounds
but they never mention
the scars it leaves behind
i wear mine
like a cloak
a reminder of love lost
and lessons learned
every tear
every heartbreak
has shaped me
into who i am now
stronger
wiser
still hopeful

82. Parents

in their eyes
i found
the kind of love
that never falters
never fades
they held me close
when the world
felt too heavy
whispering
you are enough
you are loved
and in their embrace
i found the strength
to face the storms
knowing i was never alone

83. Regrets

Sweet little baby girl
Had the world in my feet
Before I could even stand
Cradled me in your right and left hand
A precious bundle of unmade plans
Hopes and dreams of bigger things
A bright future so it seemed
Oh, but that light grew a little less bright
As I grew and we began to fight
When I was 13, I was so damn mean
Running away, had nothing more to say
Than I hate you
But that's not true now
I just don't, I just don't know how to say

84. Anxiety

some days
the weight of the world
sits heavy
on my chest
breathing becomes
a struggle
and my mind
a battlefield

85. Your not alone

loneliness settles
like dust
coating every surface
emptiness echoes
through vacant rooms
once filled with laughter
memories linger
faded photographs
tear-stained remnants
heartbreak leaves scars
invisible to others
but carved deep within
if this resonates
know you're not alone
in the depths of sorrow

86. Petals and Thorns

i was a garden
blooming
until your hands
pulled out my petals
one by one
leaving only
the thorns.

87. Chains of Words

your words
were the chains
around my soul
holding me captive
in the prison
of your anger
i learned to smile
through the pain.

88. False Love

you called it love
but love
does not bruise
does not break
does not leave scars
that never fade
you called it love
but i know
it was control.

89. Pieces of Me

each day
i stitched together
the pieces of myself
you tore apart
hoping
one day
i would be whole again.

90. Enemy in the Mirror

the mirror
became my enemy
reflecting
the shadows of your abuse
etched deep
into my skin
into my heart.

91. Extinguished Flame

i was a flame
bright and fierce
until you came
with your storm
extinguishing
every bit of light
i had left.

92. Behind Closed Doors

for even the bitterest tears,

can leave a glistening path,

a map to the honey waiting within.

behind closed doors

your true face

emerged

a monster

wearing the mask

of love

i learned

to fear.

93. Echoes of Silence

the silence
after your rage
was the loudest
scream
i ever heard
it echoed
inside my bones.

94. Invisible Ink

i wrote my pain
in invisible ink
on the pages
of my life
hoping
someone would read
and understand
the words
i could not speak.

95. Broken Wings

freedom
was a distant dream
a whisper
in the night
i chased
with broken wings
until i learned
to fly again.

96. Labyrinth of Deception

your love

was a labyrinth

each turn

a trap

each path

a dead end

i wandered

lost

in your deception.

97. Invisible Marks

your hands
left marks
not visible
to the eye
but etched
into my soul
where no one
could see.

98. Unescapable Storm

you were
a storm
i couldn't escape
lightning striking
with every word
thunder
with every blow.

99. Mask of Pretence

i wore
the mask
you gave me
pretending
everything was fine
while inside
i was crumbling.

100. Vocal Cage

your voice
a constant reminder
of the cage
you built
around my heart
each syllable
a lock
on my freedom.

101. Drowning in Waves

i was the ocean
vast and deep
you tried
to drown me
in my own waves
but i learned
to swim.

102. Poisoned Lies

your lies
were the poison
i drank
daily
slowly eroding
my sense
of self.

103. Reflections

i wear a smile
to hide the cracks
but underneath
the surface
i am a shattered
mirror
reflecting
nothing but pain.

104. Heavy Heart

the weight
of the world
rests on my chest
each breath
a struggle
each heartbeat
a reminder
of my despair.

105. Mind Prison

i am a prisoner

in my own mind

trapped

by the chains

of my thoughts

each one

a link

in the unbreakable

bond.

106. Before i go

Body sideways, teenage lightweights, dancing round the streets
Friday nights are burning brighter, another memory
Something I could hold onto when I'm missing your face
When I can hear somebody else calling your name
But you wouldn't know you got me feeling this way oh oh.

107. I'm never alone

It's crazy, my thoughts start racing
And my mind's erasing everything I knew
It's just pills and therapy bills
Just to keep me away from you
And it works for a little while, bullshit smiles
But I'm just walking through the motions
Either that, or losing track of my emotions
4 a.m. panic attacks
Taking red eyes back home
I feel by myself but with you, I'm never alone
Damn

108. Honeycomb Scars

The honeycombs that held my dreams,

now marred by shadows,

sticky with a fear I can't sweeten,

each hexagon a fractured memory,

of a world that felt safe,

a violation etched deep,

like the angry scrawl of a wasp,

the buzzing in my ears,

not the melody of creation,

but the echo of a power misused,

yet, within the broken comb,

a sliver of gold still shines,

a flicker of hope,

that I can rebuild,

stronger, wiser,

the honey I make now,

laced with the tang of salt,

a testament to the tears I've cried,

but also, a symbol of resilience,

of a spirit unbroken,

and a sweetness that will rise again.

109. Stone cold

Stone cold, stone cold
You're dancing with her, while I'm staring at my phone
Stone cold, stone cold
I was your amber, but now she's your shade of gold

110. Couple of kids

When I'm wrapped in your arms, I never feel a thing
Living life on a whim, it's never a routine
And it's troubling to live this way
When you never know where you'll stay
But we live, and we learn, and I wouldn't change a thing

111. baby dont cut

She's only 17, her whole life's ahead of her
She hates school because the people there discredit her
Her boyfriend tries to show her that's not how it seems
But everyday she just gets lowered with her self-esteem
He let's her know that every night will have a brighter day
She even tried to overdose and take her life away
She's feeling hopeless there just sitting down beside her bed
Then he takes his hand and places it beside her head
He tries to hold her but with every touch she still resists
And then he sees the scars that bury deep within her wrists
She's feeling numb, he tries to beg and plead and ask her,
"Why?"
She says this way she has control of the pain she feels inside
He's asking her, "How long it's going since you've felt this?
Way because you got me here, just feeling so damn helpless"
She says, "It's been a while. I guess I needed better luck"
And then he screams at her and tells her, "Baby, never cut!"
The next day at school she's feeling better than the day before
Even cracked a couple smiles as she walked the corridor
But all that seemed to end, she dropped her books when she
walked into class
And every student in the room just seemed to point and laugh
She couldn't take it anymore, she sent her boy a text

She said, "I love you with my body, heart and soul to death"
He thought nothing, typed "I love you", then he sent it
By "death" he didn't know that she had literally just meant it
She ducked the next class, ran home into the bathroom
Thought to herself she wouldn't break her promise that soon
One cut, two cuts, three cuts, four
The blood just started dripping from the tub to the floor
Her boyfriend had a feeling in his stomach that he hated
He followed it right down to her house he never waited
The front door was open, he heard the water running
He stormed into the bathroom and his heart just started gunning
He puts her arm around his shoulder, he's just tryna lean her back up
Yelling out her name as he lays her beside the bathtub
Feels his whole world just took a hit from a big avalanche
Screaming out so heavily, "Somebody call an ambulance!"
Feeling mad angry like somebody's led her onto this
Her eyeballs are rolling, drifting out of consciousness
Thinking to himself why the hell did she just stop at will
The tears just keep on rolling as they head to the hospital
Paramedics rush her in, the doctor calls emergency
She's lost a lot of blood the place looks like a murder scene
An hour later, the doc walks over with a sour face
And says, "Excuse me for the words that I'm about to say
I'm sorry for your loss" the boy just starts collapsing
His own world, his own girl just took a crashing

Saying to himself that it's his fault and that he let it up
"Baby, I thought you made a promise you would never cut"

112. Salt & Honey

salt,

stinging kiss on open wounds,

tears i couldn't cry, you draw them out.

honey,

golden soothe on raw tongue,

bittersweet reminder of what's sweet.

life, a dance,

they say.

but some days, my steps are salt-crusted,

others, honey-dipped.and in the space between,

a woman learns to heal,

to find sweetness in the sting,

strength in the soothe.

for even the bitterest tears,

can leave a glistening path,

a map to the honey waiting within.